Refreshing Raitas

Refreshing Raitas

DR SANDEEP MALIK & DR SANJEEV KUMAR

PARTRIDGE

A Penguin Random House Company

ISBN: Softcover   978-1-4828-4648-5
               eBook   978-1-4828-4647-8

Print information available on the last page.

To order additional copies of this book, contact
Partridge India
000 800 10062 62
orders.india@partridgepublishing.com

www.partridgepublishing.com/india

Preface / About the Book

Indian food is very revered worldwide for its variety, tastes and colours. But for many novices, Indian cuisine is synonymous to curry. This book tries to break this jink by introducing 'Raita' to readers, it is simple yet easy to prepare and delicious curd based dish. A Raita is supposed to provide relief from the spicy gravies along with adding richness to the food. Raita, like any other Indian food, varies enormously thanks to the number of ingredients available in local Indian market round the year. Most of the Raitas are very common; whereas some are very-very unusual and rare. Authors tried to include at least few of each type of Raitas with main aim to familiarise readers with art of preparing Indian food.

Introduction

'*Raita*' is not an English word neither it has any English equivalent. It is an indispensible part of Indian menu. The main purpose of *raita* is to relive a person form the hot and spicy dishes of Indian Cuisine. These are generally bland, or salty; but can be sweet too depending upon the type of main dish and personal likings.

A raita has following components:

1. ***Base*** i.e. most preferably curd otherwise buttermilk will also do. Raita made with curd will have a thicker consistency whereas the buttermilk will produce a thinner dish. Curd must be whisked well before making raita. Ideally, its texture should be thick and creamy

2. ***Main ingredient or body***: It is the most important part of the raita. From this ingredient, the raita get its name. It can be anything depending on your imagination and quest for trying new combinations with curd.

3. ***Seasonings:*** The main role of seasonings is to bring out the flavour and taste of different ingredients. Table Salt and Chilli Powder are two natural seasonings for any raita. However, different types of salt can be added to impart more flavour and variations in taste.

4. ***Spices & Herbs:*** A wide range of spices such as roasted cumin seeds, black and white pepper powder, asafoetida, cardamom powder etc may be added to increase taste, nutritional and medicinal value of a raita. Selection of spices will depend on the main ingredient.

However, it must be kept in mind that spices should not overwhelm the taste of curd and ingredients, but to support their taste.

Herbs such as mint, coriander, basil, and fenugreek leaves etc may be used, sparingly, to flavour and garnish, as well.

5. ***Garnishes:*** Garnishes serve the purpose of enhancing eye appeal of raita. However, for raita, garnish can be mixed with it or paced on the top of the finished dish. But it should be of bite size or even small, less chewy and simple; so that the guest may easily sip the raita, if desires. For a raita, small pieces of fruits, cooked vegetables, herbs, dry fruits etc can serve as garnishes.

A raita is always served as a part of main dish or course i.e. an accompaniment. It can never be served as main dish mainly due to its serving size and lightness; however, people on weight management diets can benefit themselves by making and eating a wholesome raita which will provide them a healthy meal full in various proteins, vitamins, minerals and fibers. These can be served as a separate course and that is why are priced separately in Indian menus at food and beverage selling outlets.

Classification

Raitas can be categorised as following:

> Fruit Raita
> Vegetable Raita
> Pulses Raita
> Cereal Raita
> Non-Vegetable Raita
> Sweet Raita
> Miscellaneous Raita

Contents

Aaloo Ka Raita

*(A very delicious and easy to make raita and can
be had with a number of dishes.)*

For 4 persons

Ingredients	Quantity
• Potato	03 medium sized
• Curd	03 cup
• Water	150 ml
• Salt	To taste
• Black Salt	To taste
• Powdered Red Chillies	¼ tea spoon
• Cumin Seeds	½ tea spoon
• Green Chillies	02 no.
• Coriander Leaves	Few sprigs

Method:

➢ Wash and cut potatoes into quarters.
➢ Boil in adequate water until soft and leave to cool.
➢ Meanwhile, add salt and black salt to the curd and beat curd along with water until smooth.
➢ Roast cumin seeds on hot tawa/pan until nice brown in colour and crush coarsely.
➢ Remove from fire and crush.
➢ Wash and finely chop green chillies and coriander leaves, separately.

➢ De-skin boiled potatoes and mash well.

➢ Add mashed potatoes with the curd mixture and mix well.

➢ Add half of the roasted cumin seed powder, chopped coriander leaves and green chillies to the curd mixture.

➢ Serve garnished with remaining roasted cumin seed powder, chopped coriander leaves and green chillies.

Variations: A table spoon of imli chutney can be added to give tanginess to the raita.

Note: A very rich source of carbohydrates and refreshing in summer season.

Baigan Ka Raita

(A very unusual but healthy raita)

For 4 persons

Ingredients	Quantity
• Brinjal (*Baigan*, round shaped)	01 medium sized
• Curd	03 cup
• Water	100 ml
• Salt	To taste
• Asafoetida (*Hing*)	A pinch
• Black Salt	To taste
• Green Chillies	02 no.
• Powdered Red Chillies	¼ tea spoon
• Black pepper	¼ tea spoon
• Green Chillies	02 no.
• Coriander Leaves	Few sprigs

Method:

➢ Wash and dry roast brinjal on open fire until well done.

➢ Remove outer skin and check for any pests.

➢ Leave them to cool.

➢ Meanwhile, add salt and black salt to the curd and beat curd along with water until smooth.

➢ Wash and finely chop green chillies and coriander leaves.

➢ Roast black Pepper and asafoetida on hot tawa/pan and make powder and crush coarsely.

➢ Mash the cooled brinjal well.

➢ Add mashed brinjal with the curd mixture and mix well.

➢ Add half of the roasted black pepper, asafoetida powder, coriander leaves, green chillies and powdered red chillies to the curd mixture and mix well.

➢ Serve garnished with remaining black pepper and Asafoetida powder, chopped coriander leaves and green chillies.

Variations: Add a table spoon of mint coriander chutney.

Note: A very rich source of potassium, dietary fibre and Iron.

Kela (Banana) Raita

(A very-very tasty and healthy raita.)

For 4 persons

Ingredients	Quantity
• Ripened Banana	02
• Curd	03 cup
• Water	150 ml
• Salt	To taste
• Black Salt	To taste
• Powdered Red Chillies	¼ tea spoon
• Black pepper powder	¼ tea spoon
• Green Chillies	02 no's
• Coriander Leaves	Few sprigs

Method:

- ➢ Remove outer skin of bananas.
- ➢ Mash well in a bowl.
- ➢ Meanwhile, add salt, black salt, red chilli powder and half of black pepper powder to the curd and beat along with water until smooth.
- ➢ Wash and finely chop green chillies and coriander leaves.
- ➢ Add mashed bananas with the curd mixture and mix well.
- ➢ Add half of the coriander leaves and green chillies to the curd mixture.

➢ Serve garnished with remaining black Pepper and Asafoetida powder, coriander leaves and green chillies.

Variations: Add a table spoon of mint- coriander chutney.

Note: A very rich source of potassium, dietary fibre and Iron.

Bathue Ka Raita

(A taste of Haryana.)

For 4 persons

Ingredients	Quantity
• *Bathua* Leaves	02 Bunches
• Curd	02 cup
• Water	150 ml
• Salt	To taste
• Black Salt	To taste
• Powdered Red Chillies	¼ tea spoon
• Green Chillies	02 no.
• Cumin Seeds	½ tea spoon

Method:

- ➤ Remove any inedible part of *bathua* leaves.
- ➤ Rinse in running cold water until free from soil.
- ➤ Boil with the help 50 ml water till well done (use water mentioned in recipe).
- ➤ Leave to cool and mash or chop well. Keep the water.
- ➤ Meanwhile, add salt, black salt and red chilli powder to the curd and beat along with water until smooth.
- ➤ Wash and finely chop green chillies.
- ➤ Roast cumin seeds on hot tawa/pan until nice brown in colour and crush coarsely.

➢ Mix half of the roasted cumin seeds and mashed *bathua leaves* in beaten curd.

➢ Serve garnished with remaining roasted cumin seeds.

Variations: Add a table spoon of sweet imli chutney.

Note: A very rich source of Iron and good for eyesight.

Boondi Ka Raita

(Widely eaten and very versatile raita)

For 4 persons

Ingredients	Quantity
• Raita Boondi	50 gm
• Curd	02 cup
• Water	150 ml
• Salt	To taste
• Black Salt	To taste
• Powdered Red Chillies	¼ tea spoon
• Cumin Seeds	½ tea spoon
• Green Chillies	02 nos.
• Coriander Leaves	Few sprigs, each
• Mint Leaves	Few sprigs, each

Method:

➤ Soak boondi in warm water for 3-5 minutes.

➤ Meanwhile, add salt, black salt and red chilli powder to the curd and beat along with water until smooth.

➤ Strain and press boondis gently to remove excess of water.

➤ Wash and finely chop green chillies, coriander and mint leaves.

➤ Roast cumin seeds on hot tawa/pan until nice brown in colour and crush coarsely.

> ➢ Mix half of the roasted cumin seeds, finely chop green chillies, coriander and mint leaves with curd mixture.
> ➢ Serve garnished with remaining roasted cumin seeds finely chop green chillies, coriander and mint leaves.

Variations:
- Flavoured boondis may be used.
- Coloured boondis may be used

Note: Best when served chilled.

Cucumber Raita

(Thrust quenching)

For 4 persons

Ingredients	Quantity
• Cucumber	1 medium sized piece
• Curd	02 cup
• Water	150 ml
• Salt	To taste
• Black Salt	To taste
• Green Chillies	02 no.
• Red Chilli Powder	¼ tea spoon
• Cumin Seeds	½ tea spoon
• Coriander Leaves	Few sprigs

Method:

➢ Wash and peel cucumber. Check and remove bitterness, if required.

➢ Grate or chop very finely.

➢ Add salt and black salt to the curd and beat curd along with water until smooth.

➢ Wash and finely chop green chillies and coriander leaves.

➢ Roast cumin seeds on hot tawa/pan until nice brown in colour and crush coarsely.

➢ Mix half of the roasted cumin seeds, finely chop green chillies with curd mixture and grated cucumber.

➢ Serve chilled garnished with remaining roasted cumin seeds, finely chop green chillies, and coriander leaves.

Variations:

- Don't use un-peeled cucumber

Note:

- If seeds are hard, these should be discarded.

Mint Raita

(Summers delight)

For 4 persons

Ingredients	Quantity
• Mint Leaves	15 grams
• Curd	02 cup
• Water	150 ml
• Salt	To taste
• Black Salt	To taste
• Powdered Sugar	2 tbsp
• Green Chillies	02 no.
• Powdered Red Chillies	¼ tea spoon
• Cumin Seeds	½ tea spoon

Method:

➤ Pluck and wash mint leaves and let them drain.

➤ Chop mint leaves finely.

➤ Wash and finely chop green chillies and coriander leaves.

➤ Roast cumin seeds on hot tawa/pan until nice brown in colour and crush coarsely.

➤ Mix salt, black salt, sugar and red chillies to the curd and beat along with water until smooth.

➤ Mix half of the roasted cumin seeds, finely chop green chillies with curd mixture and chopped mint leaves.

➢ Serve chilled garnished with remaining roasted cumin seeds finely chop green chillies and coriander leaves.

Variations: Serve garnished with red imli sweet and sour chutney.

Note: Very useful for upset stomach.

Cucumber & Mint Raita

(A must have in summers)

For 4 persons

Ingredients	Quantity
• Cucumber	1 medium sized piece
• Mint	20 gm
• Curd	02 cup
• Water	150 ml
• Salt	To taste
• Black Salt	To taste
• Green Chillies	02 no.
• Powdered Red Chillies	¼ tea spoon
• Cumin Seeds	½ tea spoon

Method:

➤ Wash and peel cucumber. Check and remove bitterness, if required.

➤ Wash plucked mint leaves and drain them completely.

➤ Reserve few for garnishing and chop rest finely.

➤ Wash and finely chop green chillies.

➤ Add salt and black salt to the curd and beat curd along with water until smooth.

➤ Roast cumin seeds on hot tawa/pan until nice brown in colour and crush coarsely.

> ➤ Mix half of the roasted cumin seeds, finely chop green chillies with curd mixture and add chopped cucumber and mint.
> ➤ Serve chilled garnished with remaining roasted cumin seeds, finely chop green chillies, and mint leaves.

Variations: Mint paste and grated cucumber may be used.

Note: Rich in vitamin A & C.

Tomato Raita

(Very eye appealing)

For 4 persons

Ingredients	Quantity
• Tomato	2 medium sized
• Curd	02 cup
• Water	150 ml
• Salt	To taste
• Black Salt	To taste
• Powdered Red Chillies	¼ tea spoon
• Green Chillies	02 no.
• Cumin Seeds	½ tea spoon
• Coriander Leaves	Few sprigs

Method:

➤ Wash and blanch tomatoes by dipping in boiling water for 1-2 minutes.

➤ Drain and let it cool.

➤ Remove skins, discard seeds and reserve the flesh

➤ Grate or chop very fine.

➤ Add salt, black salt and powdered red chillies to the curd and beat along with water until smooth.

➤ Wash and finely chop green chillies and coriander leaves.

➢ Roast cumin seeds on hot tawa/pan until nice brown in colour and crush them coarsely.

➢ Mix half of, each, roasted cumin seeds and finely chopped green chillies with curd mixture and chopped tomato.

➢ Serve chilled garnished with remaining roasted cumin seeds, finely chop green chillies, and coriander leaves.

Variations: Small pieces or wedges of tomatoes may be used instead of grated or chopped.

Note: A good source of Vitamin A.

Cucumber & Tomato Raita

(Very tasty and tangy raita)

For 4 persons

Ingredients	Quantity
• Cucumber	1 medium sized piece
• Tomato	1 medium
• Curd	02 cup
• Water	150 ml
• Salt	To taste
• Black Salt	To taste
• Green Chillies	02 no.
• Powdered Red Chillies	¼ tea spoon
• Coriander Leaves	2-4 sprigs

Method:

➢ Wash and peel cucumber. Check and remove bitterness, if required.

➢ Wash tomato.

➢ Blanch tomato in boiling water for 1-2 minutes.

➢ Drain and let it cool. Peel skin, discard seeds and reserve flesh.

➢ Grate or chop very finely.

➢ Add salt and black salt to the curd and beat curd along with water until smooth.

➢ Wash and finely chop green chillies.

➢ Wash green coriander and pluck leaves from stem.

- ➢ Chop leaves finely.
- ➢ Mix Cucumber, Tomato and curd mixture with finely chopped green chillies.
- ➢ Serve chilled, garnished with red chillies and coriander leaves.

Variations:

- Cubes of cucumber and tomato may be used.
- Seeds of cucumber may be discarded.

Note: Goes very well with full Indian meal.

Maruah (Basil leaves) Ka Raita

(provide resistant to various infections)

For 4 persons

Ingredients	Quantity
Basil Leaves	15 grams
Curd	02 cup
Water	150 ml
Salt	To taste
Black Salt	To taste
Powdered Sugar	2 tbsp
Black Pepper Powder	¼ tea spoon
Cumin Seeds	½ tea spoon

Method:

➢ Pluck and wash basil leaves and drain well
➢ Chop finely.
➢ Add salt, black salt, sugar and black pepper powder to the curd and beat curd along with water until smooth.
➢ Roast cumin seeds on hot tawa/pan until nice brown in colour and crush coarsely.
➢ Mix half of the roasted cumin seeds with curd mixture and chopped mint leaves.
➢ Serve chilled garnished with remaining roasted cumin seeds.

Note: Very useful for upset stomach.

Palak Ka Raita

(iron rich raita)

For 4 persons

Ingredients	Quantity
• Palak (Spinach) Leaves	02 Bunches
• Curd	02 cup
• Water	150 ml
• Salt	To taste
• Black Salt	To taste
• Green Chillies	02 no.
• Powdered Red Chillies	¼ tea spoon
• Cumin Seeds	½ tea spoon

Method:

> ➤ Wash leaves well; and remove any hard stems of palak leaves.
> ➤ Boil with the help of very little water till well done.
> ➤ Leave to cool and mash or chop well.
> ➤ Meanwhile, add salt and black salt to the curd and beat curd along with water until smooth.
> ➤ Wash and finely chop green chillies.
> ➤ Roast cumin seeds on hot tawa/pan until nice brown in colour and crush them coarsely.

➢ Mix half of the roasted cumin seeds and mashed palak leaves in beaten curd.

➢ Serve garnished with remaining roasted cumin seeds.

Note: Rich source of Iron

Cholai Ka Raita

(popularly known as Amranth)

For 4 persons

Ingredients	Quantity
• Cholai (Amaranth) Leaves	02 Bunches (250 gms)
• Curd	02 cup
• Water	150 ml
• Salt	To taste
• Black Salt	To taste
• Green Chillies	02 no.
• Powdered Red Chillies	¼ tea spoon
• Cumin Seeds	½ tea spoon

Method:

> ➢ Wash cholai leaves well in running cold water and remove any hard stems of cholai leaves.
> ➢ Boil with the help of little water till well done.
> ➢ Leave to cool and mash or chop well.
> ➢ Meanwhile, add salt and black salt to the curd and beat curd along with water until smooth.
> ➢ Wash and finely chop green chillies.

➢ Roast cumin seeds on hot tawa/pan until nice brown in colour and crush them coarsely.

➢ Mix half of the roasted cumin seeds and mashed cholai leaves in beaten curd.

➢ Serve garnished with remaining roasted cumin seeds.

Note: Believed to be having amazing healing power of nature.

Methi Leaves Ka Raita

(a tonic for heart)

For 4 persons

Ingredients	Quantity
• Methi (Fenugreek) Leaves	02 Bunches (250 gms)
• Curd	02 cup
• Water	150 ml
• Salt	To taste
• Black Salt	To taste
• Green Chillies	02 no.
• Powdered Red Chillies	¼ tea spoon
• Cumin Seeds	½ tea spoon

Method:

> ➤ Wash methi leaves well in running cold water; pluck leaves and remove any hard stems.
> ➤ Boil with the help of little water till well done.
> ➤ Leave to cool and mash or chop well.
> ➤ Meanwhile, add salt and black salt to the curd and beat curd along with water until smooth.
> ➤ Wash and finely chop green chillies.
> ➤ Roast cumin seeds on hot tawa/pan until nice brown in colour.

➤ Mix half of the roasted cumin seeds and mashed methi leaves in beaten curd.

➤ Serve garnished with remaining roasted cumin seeds.

Note: helps to reduce cholesterol level and lowers the risk of heart diseases.

Hari Chutni Ka Raita

(a tasty and tangy raita)

For 4 persons

Ingredients	Quantity
• Green Coriander Leaves	02 Bunches (250 gms)
• Mint Leaves	1 bunch (100 gms)
• Green Chillies	04 nos
• Curd	02 cup
• Water	150 ml
• Salt	To taste
• Black Salt	To taste
• Powdered Red Chillies	¼ tea spoon
• Cumin Seeds	½ tea spoon

Method:

➤ Pluck and wash coriander and mint leaves well in running cold water and remove any hard stem.

➤ Make paste of coriander and mint leaves with green chillies.

➤ Meanwhile, add salt and black salt to the curd and beat curd along with water until smooth.

➤ Roast cumin seeds on hot tawa/pan until nice brown in colour.

➤ Mix half of the roasted cumin seeds and paste of coriander-mint leaves and green chillies in beaten curd.

➤ Serve garnished with remaining roasted cumin seeds.

Variations: Sugar may be added to balance the fiery taste of chillies.

Sarson (Green Mustard plant) Ka Raita

(rich in antioxidants)

For 4 persons

Ingredients	Quantity
• Sarson Leaves	250 gm
• Curd	02 cup
• Water	150 ml
• Salt	To taste
• Black Salt	To taste
• Green Chillies	02 no.
• Powdered Red Chillies	¼ tea spoon
• Cumin Seeds	½ tea spoon

Method:

➢ Wash sarson leaves well in running cold water and remove any hard stems.

➢ Boil with the help of little water till well done.

➢ Leave to cool and mash or chop well.

➢ Meanwhile, add salt and black salt to the curd and beat curd along with water until smooth.

➢ Wash and finely chop green chillies.

➢ Roast cumin seeds on hot tawa/pan until nice brown in colour.

➤ Mix half of the roasted cumin seeds and mashed sarson leaves in beaten curd.

➤ Serve garnished with remaining roasted cumin seeds.

Note: Sarson/mustard leaves are loaded with vitamin A,C & E.

Saag Ka Raita

(a Punjabi delicacy)

For 4 persons

Ingredients	Quantity
• Sarson Leaves, Methi, Cholai and Palak Leaves	250 gm
• Curd	02 cup
• Water	150 ml
• Salt	To taste
• Black Salt	To taste
• Green Chillies	02 no.
• Powdered Red Chillies	¼ tea spoon
• Cumin Seeds	½ tea spoon

Method:

➢ Wash all leaves well in running cold water and remove any hard stems and discard spoiled leaves.

➢ Boil with the help of very less water till well done.

➢ Leave to cool and mash or chop well.

➢ Meanwhile, add salt and black salt to the curd and beat curd along with water until smooth.

➢ Wash and finely chop green chillies.

➢ Roast cumin seeds on hot tawa/pan until nice brown in colour.

➤ Mix half of the roasted cumin seeds and mashed saag leaves in beaten curd.

➤ Serve garnished with remaining roasted cumin seeds.

Note: should be eaten frequently in winter preferably during lunch time.

Kondra Ka Raita

(Kondra - a Haryanavi wild plant with edible leaves)

For 4 persons

Ingredients	Quantity
• Santhi Leaves	200 gm
• Curd	02 cup
• Water	150 ml
• Salt	To taste
• Black Salt	To taste
• Green Chillies	02 no.
• Powdered Red Chillies	¼ tea spoon
• Cumin Seeds	½ tea spoon

Method:

➢ Rinse and wash kondra leaves well.

➢ Boil with the help of little water till well done.

➢ Leave to cool and mash or chop well.

➢ Meanwhile, add salt and black salt to the curd and beat curd along with water until smooth.

➢ Wash and finely chop green chillies.

➢ Roast cumin seeds on hot tawa/pan until nice brown in colour and crush these coarsely.

➢ Mix half of the roasted cumin seeds and mashed kondra leaves in beaten curd.

➢ Serve garnished with remaining roasted cumin seeds.

Santhi Ka Raita

(An established tonic for liver diseases)

For 4 persons

Ingredients	Quantity
• Kondra Leaves	200 gm
• Curd	02 cup
• Water	150 ml
• Salt	To taste
• Black Salt	To taste
• Green Chillies	02 no.
• Powdered Red Chillies	¼ tea spoon
• Cumin Seeds	½ tea spoon

Method:

> ➢ Rinse and wash santhi leaves well.
> ➢ Boil with the help of very less water till well done.
> ➢ Leave to cool and mash or chop well.
> ➢ Meanwhile, add salt and black salt to the curd and beat curd along with water until smooth.
> ➢ Wash and finely chop green chillies.
> ➢ Roast cumin seeds on hot tawa/pan until nice brown in colour.
> ➢ Mix half of the roasted cumin seeds and mashed santhi leaves in beaten curd.
> ➢ Serve garnished with remaining roasted cumin seeds.

Sakar-Kand Ka Raita

*(A very delicious and easy to make raita and can
be had with a number of dishes.)*

For 4 persons

Ingredients	Quantity
• Sakar-Kand (Sweet potato)	03 medium sized
• Curd	03 cup
• Water	150 ml
• Salt	To taste
• Black Salt	To taste
• Cumin Seeds	½ tea spoon
• Green Chillies	02 no.
• Powdered Red Chillies	¼ tea spoon
• Coriander Leaves	Few sprigs

Method:

➢ Wash and cut sakar-kand into equal pieces.

➢ Boil until soft; drain and let them cool.

➢ Meanwhile, add salt and black salt to the curd and beat curd along
with water until smooth.

➢ Wash and finely chop green chillies and coriander leaves.

➢ Roast cumin seeds on hot tawa/pan until nice brown in colour.

➢ Remove from fire and crush cumin seeds coarsely.

➢ De-skin boiled sweet-potatoes and mash well.

> Add mashed sweet-potatoes with the curd mixture and mix well.
> Add half of the roasted cumin seed powder, coriander leaves and green chillies to the curd mixture.
> Serve garnished with remaining roasted cumin seed powder, coriander leaves and green chillies.

Variations: The sweet-potato may be roasted on slow fire and; believe us, the taste will be second to none. A table spoon of imli chutney can be added to give tanginess to the raita.

Note: A very rich source of carbohydrates and refreshing in summer season.

Dhania (Coriander) Raita

(a wonderful source of dietary fibre)

For 4 persons

Ingredients	Quantity
• Dhania Leaves	1 bunch (200 gms)
• Curd	02 cup
• Water	150 ml
• Salt	To taste
• Black Salt	To taste
• Green Chillies	02 no.
• Powdered Red Chillies	¼ tea spoon
• Cumin Seeds	½ tea spoon
• Pomegranate seeds, for garnishing	1 table spoon

Method:

➢ Rinse and wash coriander leaves well in running cold water.

➢ Pluck leaves.

➢ Boil with the help of very less water till well done.

➢ Leave to cool and make a paste.

➢ Meanwhile, add salt and black salt to the curd and beat curd along with water until smooth.

➢ Wash and finely chop green chillies.

➢ Roast cumin seeds on hot tawa/pan until nice brown in colour.

➢ Mix half of the roasted cumin seeds and coriander paste in beaten curd.

➢ Serve garnished with remaining roasted cumin seeds, pomegranate seeds and red chillies.

Variations: Boil without lid, it will give a bright colour.

Note: good for digestive system and rich source of vitamin K

Fresh Kachri Raita

(True Haryanavi flavour)

For 4 persons

Ingredients	Quantity
• Fresh Kachri	100 gm
• Curd	02 cup
• Water	150 ml
• Powdered Sugar	2 table spoon
• Salt	To taste
• Black Salt	To taste
• Green Chillies	02 no.
• Powdered Red Chillies	¼ tea spoon
• Cumin Seeds	½ tea spoon

Method:

➢ Wash kachris well.

➢ Peel, thinly, to remove the skin.

➢ Cut kachris and check the seeds. If seeds are hard, discard them. If not then these can be used.

➢ Make fine paste along with green chillies.

➢ Add salt, black salt and powdered sugar to the curd and beat curd along with water until smooth.

➢ Roast cumin seeds on hot tawa/pan until nice brown in colour and crush these coarsely.

➢ Mix half of the roasted cumin seeds and kachri paste in beaten curd.

➢ Serve garnished with remaining roasted cumin seeds and red chillies.

Dry (Shookhi) Kachri Raita

(A substitute for fresh kachri)

For 4 persons

Ingredients	Quantity
• Dried Kachri	50 gm
• Curd	02 cup
• Water	150 ml
• Powdered Sugar	2 table spoon
• Salt	To taste
• Black Salt	To taste
• Green Chillies	02 no.
• Powdered Red Chillies	¼ tea spoon
• Cumin Seeds	½ tea spoon

Method:

➢ Wash dried kachris well to remove any dirt or dust.

➢ Soak in 100 ml water for 2-3 hours.

➢ Make a paste of the soaked kachris along with green chillies.

➢ Add salt, black salt and powdered sugar to the curd and beat curd along with water until smooth.

➢ Roast cumin seeds on hot tawa/pan until nice brown in colour.

➢ Mix half of the roasted cumin seeds and dry kachri paste in beaten curd.

➢ Serve garnished with remaining roasted cumin seeds and red chillies.

Amrood ka Raita

(a poor man's apple)

For 4 persons

Ingredients	Quantity
• Amrood/Guava	250 gm
• Curd	03 cup
• Water	150 ml
• Salt	To taste
• Black Salt	To taste
• Cumin Seeds	½ tea spoon
• Green Chillies	02 no.
• Powdered Red Chillies	¼ tea spoon
• Coriander Leaves	Few sprigs

Method:

> Wash and cut guavas into quarters and remove seeds.
> If the guavas are well ripened, make a smooth paste. If guavas are hard, boil the pieces and then make paste.
> Meanwhile, add salt and black salt to the curd and beat curd along with water until smooth.
> Wash and finely chop green chillies and coriander leaves.
> Roast cumin seeds on hot tawa/pan until nice brown in colour.
> Add guava paste with the curd mixture and mix well.

➢ Add half of the roasted cumin seed powder, chopped coriander leaves and green chillies to the curd mixture.

➢ Serve garnished with remaining roasted cumin seed powder, coriander leaves and green chillies.

Note: rich source of vitamin C & dietary fibre

Lauki ka Raita

(a low calorie raita)

For 4 persons

Ingredients	Quantity
• Lauki/Bottle Gourd	500 gm
• Curd	03 cup
• Salt	To taste
• Black Salt	To taste
• Cumin Seeds	½ tea spoon
• Green Chillies	02 no.
• Powdered Red Chillies	¼ tea spoon
• Coriander Leaves	Few sprigs

Method:

- ➢ Wash, peel and cut ghiya into small pieces.
- ➢ Boil with little water till well done.
- ➢ Strain; reserve the liquid and let ghiya cool.
- ➢ Meanwhile, add salt and black salt to the curd and beat curd along with the reserved liquid until smooth.
- ➢ Wash and finely chop green chillies and coriander leaves.
- ➢ Roast cumin seeds on hot tawa/pan until nice brown in colour.
- ➢ Mash ghiya well.
- ➢ Add ghiya with the curd mixture and mix well.

➢ Add half of the roasted cumin seed powder, coriander leaves and green chillies to the curd mixture.

➢ Serve garnished with remaining roasted cumin seed powder, coriander leaves and green chillies.

Variations: instead of cutting into small pieces, ghiya can be grated

Note: rich in iron and vitamin c and B complex. Very effective against constipation and digestive disorders

Turai ka Raita

(excellent blood purifier)

For 4 persons

Ingredients	Quantity
• Turai (Indian Ridge Gourd)	500 gm
• Curd	03 cup
• Salt	To taste
• Black Salt	To taste
• Cumin Seeds	½ tea spoon
• Green Chillies	02 no.
• Powdered Red Chillies	¼ tea spoon
• Coriander Leaves	Few sprigs

Method:

➤ Wash, peel and cut torai into small pieces or grate.

➤ Boil with little water till done.

➤ Strain, reserve the liquid and let torai cool.

➤ Meanwhile, add salt and black salt to the curd and beat curd along with the reserved liquid until smooth.

➤ Wash and finely chop green chillies and coriander leaves.

➤ Mash boiled torai well.

➤ Roast cumin seeds on hot tawa/pan until nice brown in colour.

➤ Add mashed torai with the curd mixture and mix well.

- ➢ Add half of the roasted cumin seed powder, chopped coriander leaves and green chillies to the curd mixture.
- ➢ Serve garnished with remaining roasted cumin seed powder, chopped coriander leaves and green chillies.

Note: beneficial for diabetes and weight loss.

Shookhi Lal Mirch Ka Raita

(A fiery raita)

For 4 persons

Ingredients	Quantity
• Shookhi Lal Mirch (Dried whole red chillies)	3 – 4 nos.
• Curd	02 cup
• Water	150 ml
• Salt	To taste
• Black Salt	To taste
• Cumin Seeds	½ tea spoon

Method:

➢ Wash dried red chillies, well.

➢ Soak overnight in small quantity of curd and water.

➢ Grind the chillies along with the curd and make a fine paste.

➢ Add salt and black salt to the curd and beat curd along with water until smooth.

➢ Add chilli paste and mix well.

➢ Roast cumin seeds on hot tawa/pan until nice brown in colour.

➢ Mix half of the roasted cumin seeds in beaten curd.

➢ Serve garnished with remaining roasted cumin seeds.

Note: rich in vitamins and minerals but low in cholesterol

Mooli Ka Raita

(an Indian household flavour)

For 4 persons

Ingredients	Quantity
• Mooli (Radish)	2 medium sized
• Curd	02 cup
• Water	150 ml
• Salt	To taste
• Black Salt	To taste
• Green Chillies	01 no.
• Powdered Red Chillies	¼ tea spoon
• Cumin Seeds	½ tea spoon
• Coriander Leaves	Few sprigs

Method:

> Wash and remove outer skins of radishes.
> Grate very fine.
> Add salt and black salt to the curd and beat curd along with water until smooth.
> Wash and finely chop green chilli and coriander leaves.
> Roast cumin seeds on hot tawa/pan until nice brown in colour.
> Mix half of the roasted cumin seeds, finely chop green chilli and red chilli powder with curd mixture and grated radishes.
> Wash and chop green coriander leaves.

> Serve chilled garnished with remaining roasted cumin seeds, finely chop green chillies, coriander leaves and remaining red chilli powder.

Note: helps in controlling blood pressure and jaundice.

Mooli Ke Paton Ka Raita

(high in dietary fibres)

For 4 persons

Ingredients	Quantity
• Mooli/Radish Leaves	3 nos.
• Curd	02 cup
• Salt	To taste
• Black Salt	To taste
• Green Chillies	01 no.
• Powdered Red Chillies	¼ tea spoon
• Cumin Seeds	½ tea spoon
• Pomegranate seeds, for garnishing	1 table spoon

Method:

➤ Rinse and wash radish leaves well in running cold water.

➤ Boil with the help of very less water till well done, reserve the liquid.

➤ Leave to cool and make a paste or chop well.

➤ Meanwhile, add salt and black salt to the curd and beat curd along with water until smooth.

➤ Wash and finely chop green chillies.

➤ Roast cumin seeds on hot tawa/pan until nice brown in colour.

➢ Mix half of the roasted cumin seeds in beaten curd.

➢ Serve garnished with remaining roasted cumin seeds, pomegranate seeds and red chillies.

Note: Boil without lid; it will give a bright colour.

Kokum Ka Raita

(cool king of Indian fruits-kokum)

For 4 persons

Ingredients	Quantity
• Dried Kokum	5 – 6 nos.
• Curd	02 cup
• Water	150 ml
• Salt	To taste
• Black Salt	To taste
• Cumin Seeds	½ tea spoon
• Coriander Leaves	Few sprigs

Method:

➢ Wash dried kokum, well.

➢ Soak overnight in small quantity of curd and water.

➢ Grind to make a paste along with the curd.

➢ Add salt and black salt to the curd and beat curd along with water until smooth.

➢ Add kokum paste and mix well.

➢ Roast cumin seeds on hot tawa/pan until nice brown in colour.

➢ Mix half of the roasted cumin seeds in beaten curd.

➤ Wash and chop coriander leaves.

➤ Serve garnished with coriander leaves and remaining roasted cumin seeds.

Note: helps in curing piles, flatulence, constipation, heatstroke, pain, tumour etc.

Chocolate Ka Raita

(An innovative raita)

For 4 persons

Ingredients	Quantity
• Chocolate syrup	50 ml
• Curd	02 cup
• Powdered Sugar	2 table spoon
• Water	150 ml
• Chocolate Curls	30 gms

Method:

Mix all the Ingredients except chocolate curls.
Serve chilled garnished with chocolate curls

Note: rich source of antioxidants and magnesium

Singadhe Ka Raita

(a raita for vrat or fasting)

For 4 persons

Ingredients	Quantity
• Singadha/Water Chestnut	150 gm
• Curd	03 cup
• Water	150 ml
• Salt	To taste
• Black Salt	To taste
• Cumin Seeds	½ tea spoon
• Green Chillies	02 no.
• Powdered Red Chillies	¼ tea spoon
• Coriander Leaves	Few sprigs

Method:

➢ Wash and peel singadhe.

➢ Boil until soft and make a fine paste. (Otherwise paste can be made without boiling also).

➢ Meanwhile, add salt and black salt to the curd and beat curd along with water until smooth.

➢ Wash and finely chop green chillies and coriander leaves.

➢ Roast cumin seeds on hot tawa/pan until nice brown in colour.

➢ Remove from fire and crush.

➢ Add the paste with the curd mixture and mix well.

➢ Add half of the roasted cumin seed powder, coriander leaves and green chillies to the curd mixture.

➢ Serve garnished with remaining roasted cumin seed powder, coriander leaves and green chillies.

Note: rich in proteins and carbohydrates.

Kaddu Ka Raita

(beta carotene rich dish)

For 4 persons

Ingredients	Quantity
• Kaddu (Pumpkin)	500 gm
• Curd	03 cup
• Salt	To taste
• Black Salt	To taste
• Cumin Seeds	½ tea spoon
• Green Chillies	02 no.
• Powdered Red Chillies	¼ tea spoon
• Coriander Leaves	Few sprigs

Method:

➢ Wash, peel and cut pumpkin into small pieces or grate.

➢ Boil with little water till done; strain and reserve the liquid.

➢ Meanwhile, add salt and black salt to the curd and beat curd along with the reserved liquid until smooth.

➢ Wash and finely chop green chillies and coriander leaves.

➢ Mash kaddu well in a bowl.

➢ Roast cumin seeds on hot tawa/pan until nice brown in colour.

➢ Add mashed kaddu with the curd mixture and mix well.

➢ Add half of the roasted cumin seed powder, coriander leaves and green chillies to the curd mixture.

➢ Serve garnished with remaining roasted cumin seed powder, coriander leaves and green chillies.

Variations: Sweet imli chutney may be added.

Note: has antioxidant and anti-inflammatory properties

Gajjar Ka Raita

(raita based on one of the healthiest vegetable)

For 4 persons

Ingredients	Quantity
• Gajjar (Carrot)	250 gm
• Curd	03 cup
• Salt	To taste
• Black Salt	To taste
• Cumin Seeds	½ tea spoon
• Green Chillies	02 no.
• Powdered Red Chillies	¼ tea spoon
• Coriander Leaves	Few sprigs

Method:

> Wash, peel and cut carrots into small pieces or grate.
> Boil with little water till done and reserve the liquid.
> Meanwhile, add salt and black salt to the curd and beat curd along with the reserved liquid until smooth.
> Wash and finely chop green chillies and coriander leaves.
> Roast cumin seeds on hot tawa/pan until nice brown in colour.
> Mash cooled carrot.
> Add mashed carrot with the curd mixture and mix well.

➤ Add half of the roasted cumin seed powder, coriander leaves and green chillies to the curd mixture.

➤ Serve garnished with remaining roasted cumin seed powder, coriander leaves and green chillies.

Variations: Sour imli chutney may be added.

Note: keeps skin beautiful and helps in cancer prevention, and anti-aging.

Dry Fruit Raita

(very rich accompaniment)

For 4 persons

Ingredients	Quantity
• Assorted Dry Fruits (Almonds, Cashew-nuts, Pistachio)	75 gms
• Curd	02 cup
• Water	150 ml
• Salt	To taste
• Black Salt	To taste
• Green Chillies	02 no.
• Powdered Red Chillies	¼ tea spoon
• Raisins	10-15 pieces
• Cumin Seeds	½ tea spoon

Method:

➢ Soak cashew-nuts in water for 2 hours.

➢ Blanch remaining dry-fruits and remove skins.

➢ Make a fine paste of all dry fruits and keep aside.

➢ Meanwhile, add salt and black salt to the curd and beat curd along with water until smooth.

➢ Wash and finely chop green chillies.

➢ Roast cumin seeds on hot tawa/pan until nice brown in colour.

➢ Mix half of the roasted cumin seeds, chopped green chillies and dry fruit paste in beaten curd.

➢ Serve garnished with remaining roasted cumin seeds.

Note: rich in proteins and dietary fibres

Hing Ka Raita

(a doctor at home)

For 4 persons

Ingredients	Quantity
• Powdered Hing (Asafoetida)	5 gms
• Curd	02 cup
• Water	150 ml
• Salt	To taste
• Black Salt	To taste
• Green Chillies	02 no.
• Powdered Red Chillies	¼ tea spoon
• Raisins	10-15 pieces
• Cumin Seeds	½ tea spoon

Method:

➢ Add salt and black salt to the curd and beat curd along with water until smooth.

➢ Wash and finely chop green chillies.

➢ Wash and chop raisins.

➢ Roast cumin seeds on hot tawa/pan until nice brown in colour and crush these coarsely.

➢ Mix raisins, half of the roasted cumin seeds and chopped green chillies in beaten curd.

➢ Roast hing powder in a pan, when done switch off the fire and add the curd mixture. Cover immediately and leave for 3-4 minutes.

➢ Serve garnished with remaining roasted cumin seeds.

Variations: hing may be fried in small quantity of oil instead of roasting.

Note: helps in stomach pain and gastric problems.

Zeera Raita

(seed of good digestion)

For 4 persons

Ingredients	Quantity
• Zeera (Cumin Seeds)	10 gms
• Curd	02 cup
• Water	150 ml
• Salt	To taste
• Black Salt	To taste
• Green Chillies	02 no.
• Powdered Red Chillies	¼ tea spoon

Method:

➤ Add salt and black salt to the curd and beat curd along with water until smooth.

➤ Wash and finely chop green chillies.

➤ Roast cumin seeds on hot tawa/pan until nice brown in colour and crush these coarsely.

➤ Mix half of the roasted cumin seeds and chopped green chillies in beaten curd.

➤ Serve garnished with remaining roasted cumin seeds.

Variations: Cumin seeds may be fried in small quantity of oil instead of roasting.

Note: an immunity builder and rich in iron

Strawberry Ka Raita

(queen of fruits-strawberry)

For 4 persons

Ingredients	Quantity
• Ripened Strawberries	100 gm
• Curd	03 cup
• Water	100 ml
• Salt	To taste
• Black Salt	To taste
• Green Chilli	01 no.
• Black pepper powder	¼ tea spoon
• Mint Leaves	Few sprigs

Method:

➤ Wash and clean strawberries gently.

➤ Make puree of these with green chilli in a blender.

➤ Add salt, black salt, half of black pepper powder to the curd and beat curd along with water until smooth.

➤ Mix fruit puree with curd mixture.

➤ Serve garnished with remaining black Pepper powder and mint leaves.

Note: helps in burning unwanted fat.

Mango Raita

(king of fruits)

For 4 persons

Ingredients	Quantity
• Well Ripened Mango	250 gm
• Curd	03 cup
• Water	100 ml
• Salt	To taste
• Black Salt	To taste
• Green Chilli	01 no.
• Black pepper powder	¼ tea spoon
• Mint Leaves	Few sprigs

Method:

➢ Wash and clean mangoes with care.

➢ Remove their skins and stones. Reserve the flesh and make puree in a blender.

➢ Add salt, black salt, half of black pepper powder to the curd and beat curd along with water until smooth.

➢ Mix mango puree with curd mixture.

➢ Serve garnished with remaining black pepper powder and washed mint leaves.

Note: rich source of vitamin A, C & dietary fibres

Sitaphal Raita

(delicious taste and nutritious)

For 4 persons

Ingredients	Quantity
• Well Ripened Sitaphal	250 gm
• Curd	03 cup
• Water	100 ml
• Salt	To taste
• Black Salt	To taste
• Green Chillies	01 no.
• Black Pepper powder	¼ tea spoon
• Dry Ginger Powder	¼ tea spoon
• Mint Leaves	Few sprigs

Method:

➢ Wash and clean fruits with care.
➢ Remove their skin and stones. Reserve the flesh and make puree in a blender.
➢ Add salt, black salt, half of black pepper powder and dry ginger powder to the curd; and beat curd along with water until smooth.
➢ Mix fruit puree with curd mixture.
➢ Serve garnished with remaining black pepper powder and washed mint leaves.

Note: good for eyes, digestion and pregnant ladies.

Papaya Raita

(The Fruit of the Angels)

For 4 persons

Ingredients	Quantity
• Well Ripened Papaya	250 gm
• Curd	03 cup
• Water	100 ml
• Salt	To taste
• Black Salt	To taste
• Green Chillies	01 no.
• Black Pepper Powder	¼ tea spoon
• Mint Leaves	Few sprigs

Method:

➢ Wash and clean papaya carefully.

➢ Remove skin and seeds. Reserve the flesh and make puree in a blender.

➢ Add salt, black salt, and half of black pepper powder to the curd; and beat curd along with water until smooth.

➢ Mix papaya puree with curd mixture.

➢ Serve garnished with remaining black Pepper powder and mint leaves.

Note: good source of minerals, vitamins and enzymes

Makhane Ka Raita

(Popped Lotus Seeds)

For 4 persons

Ingredients	Quantity
• Makhane/Popped Lotus Seeds	50 gm
• Oil/fat	For frying
• Curd	03 cup
• Water	100 ml
• Salt	To taste
• Black Salt	To taste
• Green Chillies	01 no.
• Black Pepper Powder	¼ tea spoon
• Mint Leaves	Few sprigs

Method:

> ➤ Fry makhane in oil or fat till golden brown in colour.
> ➤ Leave to cool and grind well with help of small quantity of curd.
> ➤ Add salt, black salt, and half of black pepper powder to the above mixture; and beat along with water until smooth.
> ➤ Serve garnished with remaining black pepper powder.

Note: a rich source of phosphorus, protein, potassium and magnesium.

Egg Ka Raita

(a superfood raita)

For 4 persons

Ingredients	Quantity
• Boiled Eggs	4 number
• Curd	03 cup
• Water	100 ml
• Salt	To taste
• Black Salt	To taste
• Green Chillies	01 no.
• Black Pepper Powder	¼ tea spoon
• Coriander Leaves	Few sprigs

Method:

➢ Remove egg shells.

➢ Separate egg whites and yolks.

➢ Discard egg yolks and mash the egg whites well. (If you are not very conscious about calorie intake then mash whole eggs.)

➢ Add salt, black salt, half of black pepper powder to the mashed egg whites.

➢ Add curd and beat along with water until smooth.

➢ Serve garnished with remaining black pepper powder and coriander leaves.

Variations: Both egg white and yolk may also be used for preparing egg raita.

Note: an excellent source of protein.

Murmure Ka Raita

(very light raita)

For 4 persons

Ingredients	Quantity
• Murmure/puffed rice	50 gm
• Oil/fat	For frying
• Curd	03 cup
• Water	100 ml
• Salt	To taste
• Black Salt	To taste
• Green Chillies	01 no.
• Black Pepper Powder	¼ tea spoon
• Coriander Leaves	Few sprigs

Method:

➤ Fry Murmure in oil or fat till golden brown in colour. (These can be used without frying also)

➤ Leave to cool and grind well with help of small quantity of curd.

➤ Add salt, black salt, half of black pepper powder to the above mixture and beat along with water until smooth.

➤ Serve garnished with remaining black Pepper powder and coriander leaves.

Variations: Sweet murmure may be used.

Kheel Ka Raita

(another form of puffed rice)

For 4 persons

Ingredients	Quantity
• Kheel	50 gm
• Oil/fat	For frying
• Curd	03 cup
• Water	100 ml
• Salt	To taste
• Black Salt	To taste
• Green Chillies	01 no.
• Black pepper	¼ tea spoon

Method:

➢ Fry Kheel in oil or fat till golden brown in colour.

➢ Kheel can be used without frying also.

➢ Leave to cool and grind well with help of small quantity of curd.

➢ Add salt, black salt, half of black pepper powder to the above mixture and beat along with water until smooth.

➢ Serve garnished with remaining black pepper powder and coriander leaves.

Variations: Sweet variety of kheel may be used.

Apple Ka Raita

(an apple a day keeps the doctor away)

For 4 persons

Ingredients	Quantity
• Apple	1 number
• Curd	03 cup
• Water	100 ml
• Salt	To taste
• Black Salt	To taste
• Green Chillies	01 no.
• Cinnamon Powder	¼ tea spoon
• Black Pepper Powder	¼ tea spoon
• Mint Leaves	Few sprigs

Method:

➢ Add salt, black salt, half of cinnamon powder and black pepper powder to the curd; and beat curd along with water until smooth.

➢ Wash and finely chop green chillies and mint leaves.

➢ Wash, peel apple and remove seeds; and cut into quarters.

➢ Make a smooth paste using a blender and keep aside

➢ Add apple-paste with the curd mixture and mix well.

➢ Add green chillies to the curd mixture.

➢ Serve garnished with remaining cinnamon and black pepper powder, and mint leaves.

Note: very rich in minerals, vitamins and proteins.

Chicken Ka Raita

(Unusual raita)

For 4 persons

Ingredients	Quantity
• Boneless Chicken Pieces	150 gm
• Whole Spices: Bay leaf-1, Big Cardamom-1, 1/2" cinnamon stick, Black pepper-2, Cloves-2	
• Curd	03 cup
• Water	100 ml
• Salt	To taste
• Black Salt	To taste
• Green Chillies	01 no.
• Red Chilli Powder	¼ tea spoon
• Coriander Leaves	Few sprigs

Method:

- ➢ Wash the chicken pieces well to remove any blood.
- ➢ Cut into small pieces.
- ➢ Boil chicken pieces in the prescribed water with salt and whole spices till well done. Don't throw away the liquid.
- ➢ Leave it to cool and throw away the whole spices.
- ➢ Process boiled chicken and green chillies in blender with the liquid.
- ➢ Add curd, red chilli powder and process in blender until smooth.

➢ Wash and chop coriander leaves.

➢ Serve garnished with chopped coriander leaves.

Variations: two or three table spoons of leftover chicken gravy may be added to boost the taste

Note: great source of lean protein.

Mutton Ka Raita

(a typical raita)

For 4 persons

Ingredients	Quantity
• Boneless Mutton	150 gm
• Whole Spices: Bay leaf-1, Big Cardamom-1, 1/2" cinnamon stick, Black pepper-2, Cloves-2	
• Water	200 ml
• Curd	03 cup
• Salt	To taste
• Black Salt	To taste
• Green Chillies	01 no.
• Black pepper	¼ tea spoon
• Coriander Leaves	Few sprigs

Method:

➢ Clean mutton pieces in cold water. Remove any fat.

➢ Cut into small pieces.

➢ Boil mutton pieces in prescribed water with salt and whole spices till well done. Don't throw away the liquid. Leave to cool.

➢ Process boiled mutton and green chillies in blender with water.

➢ Add curd and process in blender until smooth.

➢ Wash and chop coriander leaves.

➤ Serve garnished with remaining coriander leaves.

Variations: two or three table spoons of any leftover mutton gravy may be added to boost the taste

Note: great source of lean and low fat protein.

Imli Ka Raita

(a sweet and tangy raita)

For 4 persons

Ingredients	Quantity
• Tamarind	75 gm
• Powdered Sugar	30 gm
• Curd	03 cup
• Water	150 ml
• Salt	To taste
• Black Salt	To taste
• Cumin Seeds	½ tea spoon
• Powdered Red Chillies	¼ tea spoon
• Coriander Leaves	Few sprigs

Method:

➤ Soak tamarind in hot water for 4-5 hours.

➤ Mash with hand and discard seeds and fibrous part.

➤ Mix the pulp with sugar, curd, water, salt, black salt, and powdered red chillies, well.

➤ Roast cumin seeds on hot tawa/pan until nice brown in colour and crush these coarsely.

- ➤ Add half of the roasted cumin seed powder to the curd mixture.
- ➤ Serve garnished with remaining roasted cumin seed powder and chopped green coriander leaves.

Note: a laxative, digestive, and a remedy for biliousness and bile disorders.

Cabbage Ka Raita

(cabbage-a brain food)

For 4 persons

Ingredients	Quantity
• Cabbage	½ piece
• Curd	03 cup
• Water	150 ml
• Salt	To taste
• Black Salt	To taste
• Cumin Seeds	½ tea spoon
• Powdered Red Chillies	¼ tea spoon

Method:

- ➢ Wash Cabbage and grate through fine greater
- ➢ Mix curd, water, salt, black salt, and powdered red chillies, well.
- ➢ Roast cumin seeds on hot tawa/pan until nice brown in colour and crush these coarsely.
- ➢ Add half of the roasted cumin seed powder to the curd mixture.
- ➢ Add finely grated cabbage to the curd mixture
- ➢ Serve garnished with remaining roasted cumin seed powder

Variation: grated cabbage may be slightly boiled in very less quantity of water.

Note: ideal for weight loss.

Gobhi Ka Raita

(deserves a regular rotation in your diet)

For 4 persons

Ingredients	Quantity
• Gobhi/Cauliflower	1 piece of medium size
• Curd	03 cup
• Water	150 ml
• Salt	To taste
• Black Salt	To taste
• Cumin Seeds	½ tea spoon
• Powdered Red Chillies	¼ tea spoon

Method:

- ➢ Wash cauliflower, remove hard stems and leaves.
- ➢ Check for pests (if any) and grate through fine greater.
- ➢ Mix curd, water, salt, black salt, and powdered red chillies, well.
- ➢ Roast cumin seeds on hot tawa/pan until nice brown in colour and crush these coarsely.
- ➢ Add half of the roasted cumin seed powder to the curd mixture.
- ➢ Add finely grated cauliflower to the curd mixture
- ➢ Serve garnished with remaining roasted cumin seed powder

Variations: Cauliflower may be boiled and mashed for making raita.

Note: contains a wide range of nutrients, including vitamins, minerals, antioxidants, and other phytochemicals and has also shown anti-cancer effects.

Bread Ka Raita-1

(very easy to make)

For 4 persons

Ingredients	Quantity
• Bread	3 slices
• Curd	03 cup
• Water	150 ml
• Salt	To taste
• Black Salt	To taste
• Cumin Seeds	½ tea spoon
• Powdered Red Chillies	¼ tea spoon

Method:

- ➤ Remove the curst of breads.
- ➤ Cut bread into 1 cm size dice.
- ➤ Fry the dices in hot oil until golden brown in colour
- ➤ Drain out excess oil and leave them to cool.
- ➤ Mix curd, water, salt, black salt, and powdered red chillies, well.
- ➤ Roast cumin seeds on hot tawa/pan until nice brown in colour and crush these coarsely.
- ➤ Add half of the roasted cumin seed powder to the curd mixture.
- ➤ Add fried bread to the curd mixture
- ➤ Serve garnished with remaining roasted cumin seed powder

Note: very easy to digest.

Bread Ka Raita-2

(simple yet tasty)

For 4 persons

Ingredients	Quantity
• Bread	3 slices
• Curd	03 cup
• Water	150 ml
• Salt	To taste
• Black Salt	To taste
• Cumin Seeds	½ tea spoon
• Powdered Red Chillies	¼ tea spoon

Method:

➢ Remove the curst of breads.

➢ Cut bread into 1 cm size dice.

➢ Mix curd, water, salt, black salt, and powdered red chillies, well.

➢ Roast cumin seeds on hot tawa/pan until nice brown in colour and crush these coarsely.

➢ Add half of the roasted cumin seed powder to the curd mixture.

➢ Add bread pieces to the curd mixture

➢ Serve garnished with remaining roasted cumin seed powder

Note: can be excellent baby food.

Biscuit Ka Raita

(A joy for kids)

For 4 persons

Ingredients	Quantity
• Biscuit (sweet/salty or both)	10 numbers
• Curd	03 cup
• Water	150 ml
• Salt	To taste
• Black Salt	To taste
• Cumin Seeds	½ tea spoon
• Powdered Red Chillies	¼ tea spoon

Method:

➢ Roast cumin seeds on hot tawa/pan until nice brown in colour and crush these coarsely.

➢ Blend curd with biscuits in a blender.

➢ Add water and again blend well.

➢ Mix salt, black salt, and powdered red chillies to the curd mixture.

➢ Add half of the roasted cumin seed powder to the curd mixture.

➢ Serve garnished with remaining roasted cumin seed powder

Variations: flavoured biscuits may be used to give newness to the raita.

Sabudane Ka Raita

(Special Raita for fasting)

For 4 persons

Ingredients	Quantity
• Sabudana/sago pearls	50 gms
• Curd	03 cup
• Water	250 ml
• Rock Salt	To taste
• Cumin Seeds	½ tea spoon
• Green Chillies	02 no.
• Coriander Leaves	Few sprigs

Method:

> Roast cumin seeds on hot tawa/pan until nice brown in colour and crush these coarsely.
> Boil sabudana with water till done.
> Add rock salt to the curd and sabudana mixture.
> Wash and finely chop green chillies and coriander leaves.
> Add half of the roasted cumin seed powder, coriander leaves and green chillies to the curd mixture.

> ➢ Serve garnished with remaining roasted cumin seed powder, coriander leaves and green chillies.

Variations: Boiled potatoes may be added to the raita to make it more nutritious.

Note: rich in carbohydrates.

Orange Raita

(a delicious and juicy treat)

For 4 persons

Ingredients	Quantity
• Orange	2 number
• Curd	03 cup
• Water	100 ml
• Salt	To taste
• Black Salt	To taste
• Green Chillies	01 no.
• Black Pepper Powder	¼ tea spoon
• Mint Leaves	Few sprigs

Method:

- ➤ Peel orange.
- ➤ Remove seeds and pips; reserve flesh.
- ➤ Add salt, black salt, half of black pepper powder to the curd and beat curd along with water until smooth.
- ➤ Mix the flesh with curd mixture.
- ➤ Serve garnished with remaining black pepper powder and mint leaves.

Variations: little orange juice may be added.

Note: helps in preventing kidney diseases and cancer.

Mixed Fruit Raita

(a all whether delight)

For 4 persons

Ingredients	Quantity
• Assorted Fruits (apple, banana, papaya, grapes etc.)	250 gms
• Curd	02 cup
• Water	100 ml
• Salt	To taste
• Black Salt	To taste
• Green Chillies	01 no.
• Black Pepper Powder	¼ tea spoon
• Mint Leaves	Few sprigs
• Pomegranate seeds	2 table spoons

Method:

> ➢ Prepare all the fruits i.e. remove skins, seeds or any other inedible part.
> ➢ Make a puree of fruits in a blender.
> ➢ Add salt, black salt, half of black pepper powder to the curd and beat curd along with water until smooth.
> ➢ Mix the fruit puree with curd mixture.

> ➢ Serve garnished with remaining black pepper powder, pomegranate seeds and mint leaves.

Variations: canned fruits may be used ; and instead of making puree, fruits may be finely chopped and used.

Note: contains variety of vitamins and minerals.

Sev Ka Raita

(very innovative raita)

For 4 persons

Ingredients	Quantity
• Indian Sev	100 gm
• Curd	03 cup
• Water	100 ml
• Salt	To taste
• Black Salt	To taste
• Green Chillies	01 no.
• Black Pepper Powder	¼ tea spoon
• Coriander Leaves	Few sprigs
• Pomegranate seeds	2 table spoons

Method:

➢ Add salt, black salt, half of black pepper powder to the curd and beat curd along with water until smooth.

➢ Add half of the roasted cumin seed powder, coriander leaves and green chillies to the curd mixture.

➢ Mix the sev with curd mixture.

➢ Serve garnished with remaining black pepper powder, pomegranate seeds and coriander leaves.

Kali Mirch Ka Raita

(Indian flavour)

For 4 persons

Ingredients	Quantity
• Black Pepper	½ tea spoon
• Curd	03 cup
• Water	100 ml
• Salt	To taste
• Black Salt	To taste
• Green Chillies	01 no.
• Pomegranate seeds	2 table spoons

Method:

➢ Crush black peppers coarsely.

➢ Wash and finely chop green chillies.

➢ Mix salt, black salt, half of black pepper powder to the curd and beat curd along with water until smooth.

➢ Serve garnished with remaining black pepper powder and pomegranate seeds.

Coconut Raita

(South Indian Delight)

For 4 persons

Ingredients	Quantity
• Coconut	½ piece
• Curd	03 cup
• Coconut Milk	150 ml
• Salt	To taste
• Black Salt	To taste
• Green Chillies	01 no.
• Black Pepper Powder	¼ tea spoon
• Pomegranate seeds	2 table spoons

Method:

➢ Peel and wash coconut well.

➢ Grate coconut and keep aside.

➢ Mix curd and coconut milk.

➢ Finely chop green chillies.

➢ Add salt, black salt, green chillies and half of the black pepper powder to curd mixture.

➢ Serve garnished with remaining black pepper powder and pomegranate seeds.

Note: Coconut is said to have therapeutic effects on brain disorders like epilepsy and Alzheimer's.

Coconut & Raisin Raita

(combined goodness)

For 4 persons

Ingredients	Quantity
• Coconut	¼ piece
• Raisins	15-20 nos
• Curd	03 cup
• Coconut Milk	150 ml
• Salt	To taste
• Black Salt	To taste
• Green Chillies	01 no.
• Black Pepper Powder	¼ tea spoon
• Pomegranate seeds	2 table spoons

Method:

- ➤ Peel and wash coconut well.
- ➤ Grate coconut and keep aside.
- ➤ Soak raisins till they puff up and chop coarsely.
- ➤ Mix curd and coconut milk.
- ➤ Finely chop green chillies.
- ➤ Add salt, black salt, green chillies, chopped raisins half of the black pepper powder to curd mixture.
- ➤ Serve garnished with remaining black pepper powder and pomegranate seeds.

Note: useful, especially, for summers.

Aloe Vera Raita

(promote healthy living)

For 4 persons

Ingredients	Quantity
• Aloe Vera Gel	100 ml
• Curd	03 cup
• Salt	To taste
• Black Salt	To taste
• Green Chillies	01 no.
• Black Pepper Powder	¼ tea spoon
• Mint Leaves	2 table spoons

Method:

➢ Mix Aloe Vera gel with curd and mix well.

➢ Wash and finely chop green chillies.

➢ Wash and finely chop mint leaves.

➢ Add salt, black salt, green chillies and half of the black pepper powder to curd mixture.

➢ Serve garnished with remaining black pepper powder and mint leaves.

Note: ensure healthy bowel movement giving you good digestive strength and regulates the immune system

Wheat Germ Raita

(even good for people allergic to wheat)

For 4 persons

Ingredients	Quantity
• Wheat Germ Juice	100 ml
• Curd	03 cup
• Salt	To taste
• Black Salt	To taste
• Green Chillies	01 no.
• Black pepper powder	¼ tea spoon
• Mint Leaves	2 table spoons

Method:

➢ Mix wheat germ juice with curd and mix well.

➢ Wash and finely chop green chillies.

➢ Wash and finely chop mint leaves.

➢ Add salt, black salt, green chillies and half of the black pepper powder to curd mixture.

➢ Serve garnished with remaining black pepper powder and mint leaves.

Note: rich in vitamin B complex, chlorophyll, beta carotene, and other vitamins, minerals and enzymes.

Mulberry Raita

(Refreshingly succulent, tart and sweet mulberries)

For 4 persons

Ingredients	Quantity
• Wheat Germ Juice	100 ml
• Curd	03 cup
• Salt	To taste
• Black Salt	To taste
• Green Chillies	01 no.
• Black pepper powder	¼ tea spoon
• Mint Leaves	2 table spoons

Method:

- ➤ Wash and clean mulberries, gently.
- ➤ Discard any spoiled and inedible part.
- ➤ Reserve few mulberries and make paste of remaining in a blender.
- ➤ Wash and finely chop green chillies.
- ➤ Mix mulberry paste and curd.
- ➤ Add salt, black salt, green chillies and half of the black pepper powder to curd mixture.
- ➤ Serve garnished with remaining black pepper powder and mulberries.

Note: contains health compounds like polyphenol pigment antioxidants, minerals, and vitamins that are essential for optimum health.

Broccoli ka Raita

(hearty and tasty)

For 4 persons

Ingredients	Quantity
• Broccoli	1 piece medium sized
• Curd	03 cup
• Water	150 ml
• Salt	To taste
• Black Salt	To taste
• Cumin Seeds	½ tea spoon
• Powdered Red Chillies	¼ tea spoon

Method:

- ➢ Wash broccoli, remove hard stems and leaves.
- ➢ Check for pests (if any) and grate through fine greater.
- ➢ Mix curd, water, salt, black salt, and powdered red chillies, well.
- ➢ Roast cumin seeds on hot tawa/pan until nice brown in colour and crush coarsely.
- ➢ Add half of the roasted cumin seed powder to the curd mixture.
- ➢ Add finely grated cauliflower to the curd mixture
- ➢ Serve garnished with remaining roasted cumin seed powder

Variations: Broccoli may be boiled and mashed for further usage

Note: Have cancer fighting and immune boosting properties.

Karela Raita

(Bitter Melon/Gourd)

For 4 persons

Ingredients	Quantity
• Karela (Bitter Melon/Gourd)	1 piece medium sized
• Karela Juice	50 ml
• Curd	03 cup
• Water	50 ml
• Salt	To taste
• Black Salt	To taste
• Cumin Seeds	½ tea spoon
• Powdered Red Chillies	¼ tea spoon

Method:

- ➢ Wash karela; scrub the skin.
- ➢ Apply salt and leave for few hours.
- ➢ Wash well and boil till done.
- ➢ Drain and leave to cool.
- ➢ Mash boiled karela.
- ➢ Roast cumin seeds on hot tawa/pan until nice brown in colour and crush coarsley.

➤ Mix karela juice, curd, water, salt, black salt, and powdered red chillies, well.

➤ Add half of the roasted cumin seed powder to the curd mixture.

➤ Serve garnished with remaining roasted cumin seed powder

Note: Beneficial in lowering sugar level, cholera and Blood disorders.

Amla Raita

(a food to fitness)

For 4 persons

Ingredients	Quantity
• Amla/Indian Gooseberry	100 gm
• Curd	03 cup
• Water	100 ml
• Salt	To taste
• Black Salt	To taste
• Cumin Seeds	½ tea spoon
• Powdered Red Chillies	¼ tea spoon

Method:

- ➢ Wash amla.
- ➢ Boil till done.
- ➢ Drain and leave to cool.
- ➢ Remove seeds.
- ➢ Mash boiled amla.
- ➢ Pass through a sieve and discard the fibrous part.
- ➢ Roast cumin seeds on hot tawa/pan until nice brown in colour and crush coarsely.

➤ Mix curd, water, salt, black salt, and powdered red chillies, well.

➤ Add sieved amla paste and add half of the roasted cumin seed powder to the curd mixture.

➤ Serve garnished with remaining roasted cumin seed powder

Note: Amla is very rich source of Vitamin C

Cheeku Ka Raita

(known as sapodilla or Manilkara Zapota)

For 4 persons

Ingredients	Quantity
• Well Ripened Cheeku (Sapota)	150 gm
• Curd	03 cup
• Water	100 ml
• Salt	To taste
• Black Salt	To taste
• Green Chillies	01 no.
• Black Pepper Powder	¼ tea spoon
• Mint Leaves	Few sprigs

Method:

➢ Wash and clean the fruits with care.

➢ Remove skin and seeds.

➢ Reserve the flesh and make puree in a blender with small quantity of curd.

➢ Add salt, black salt, half of black pepper powder to the remaining curd and beat with water until smooth.

➢ Mix fruit puree with curd mixture.

➢ Serve garnished with remaining black pepper powder and mint leaves.

Note: Rich source of Vitamin A and helps in good vision

Kiwi Fruit Ka Raita

(kiwi fruit is native to northern China)

For 4 persons

Ingredients	Quantity
• Well Ripened Kiwi Fruit	100 gm
• Curd	03 cup
• Water	100 ml
• Salt	To taste
• Black Salt	To taste
• Green Chillies	01 no.
• Black pepper	¼ tea spoon
• Pomegranate Seeds	30 gms

Method:

➢ Wash and clean the fruits with care.

➢ Remove the skin.

➢ Reserve the flesh and make puree in a blender with small quantity of curd.

➢ Add salt, black salt, half of black pepper powder to the remaining curd and beat with water until smooth.

> ➢ Mix fruit puree with curd mixture.
> ➢ Serve garnished with remaining black Pepper powder and pomegranate seeds.

Note: packs in the vital nutrients vitamin E, copper, vitamin K, choline, magnesium and phosphorus

Jamun Ka Raita

(known as black plum- a summer fruit)

For 4 persons

Ingredients	Quantity
• Well Ripened Jamun	250 gm
• Curd	03 cup
• Water	100 ml
• Salt	To taste
• Black Salt	To taste
• Green Chillies	01 no.
• Black pepper	¼ tea spoon
• Mint Leaves	Few sprigs

Method:

➢ Wash and clean the fruits with care.

➢ Remove seeds and reserve the flesh.

➢ Make puree in a blender with small quantity of curd.

➢ Add salt, black salt, half of black pepper powder to the remaining curd and beat with water until smooth.

➢ Mix fruit puree with curd mixture.

➢ Serve garnished with remaining black Pepper powder and mint leaves.

Note: used to treat digestive disorders such as diarrhea, dysentery and dyspepsia.

Angoor Ka Raita

(very old fruit)

For 4 persons

Ingredients	Quantity
• Well Ripened Angoor/Grape	250 gm
• Curd	03 cup
• Salt	To taste
• Black Salt	To taste
• Green Chillies	01 no.
• Black Pepper Powder	¼ tea spoon
• Mint Leaves	Few sprigs

Method:

➢ Wash and clean the fruits with care.

➢ Remove pip.

➢ Make puree in a blender with small quantity of curd.

➢ Add salt, black salt, half of black pepper powder to the remaining curd and beat with water until smooth.

➢ Mix fruit puree with curd mixture.

➢ Serve garnished with remaining black Pepper powder and mint leaves.

Note: reduces the risk of strokes and kidney stones.

Onion Raita

(part of the allium family of vegetables and herbs)

For 4 persons

Ingredients	Quantity
• Onion	100 gm
• Curd	03 cup
• Salt	To taste
• Black Salt	To taste
• Water	100 ml
• Green Chillies	01 no.
• Red Chillies	¼ tea spoon
• Green Coriander Leaves	Few sprigs

Method:

➢ Peel and wash onions.

➢ Grate coarsely.

➢ Wash and finely chop green chillies.

➢ Wash and finely chop green coriander.

➢ Add salt, black salt, half of red chilli powder to the curd and beat with water until smooth.

- ➢ Mix grated onion and green chillies with curd mixture.
- ➢ Serve garnished with remaining red chilli powder and coriander leaves.

Note: rich in sulphur, fibers, potassium, vitamin B, vitamin C and they are low in fat, cholesterol and sodium.

Beetroot Raita

(known as table beet, garden beet, red or golden beet in North America)

For 4 persons

Ingredients	Quantity
• Beetroot	100 gm
• Curd	03 cup
• Water	100 ml
• Salt	To taste
• Black Salt	To taste
• Green Chillies	01 no.
• Black Pepper Powder	¼ tea spoon
• Mint Leaves	Few sprigs

Method:

➢ Wash and clean fruits.

➢ Remove the skin and grate.

➢ Boil till tender and strain; don't throw away the liquid.

➢ Wash and finely chop green chillies.

➢ Add salt, black salt, half of black pepper powder and chopped green chillies to the curd.

➢ Beat with water until smooth.

> ➢ Mix grated with curd mixture.
> ➢ Serve garnished with remaining black pepper powder and mint leaves.

Note: Contains potassium, magnesium and iron as well vitamins A, B6 and C, and folic acid.

Lahsun Ka Raita

(a single bulb of garlic a day, keeps diseases away)

For 4 persons

Ingredients	Quantity
• Lahsun (Garlic)	3-4 flakes
• Curd	03 cup
• Water	100 ml
• Salt	To taste
• Black Salt	To taste
• Green Chillies	01 no.
• Black Pepper Powder	¼ tea spoon
• Oil	1 tea spoon
• Coriander Leaves	Few sprigs

Method:

➢ Mix curd, well, with water, salt, black salt, half of black pepper.

➢ Wash and finely chop green chillies.

➢ Add half of the chopped green chillies with curd mixture.

➢ Peel garlic flakes.

➢ Finely chop or crush garlic.

➢ Heat oil in a pan and fry garlic flakes till light brown in colour.

➢ Remove from fire and add the curd mixture.

➤ Put lid and leave till cool.
➤ Serve garnished with remaining black pepper powder and chopped coriander leaves.

Note: Garlic is used for treating bites, tumours, ulcer, wounds, heart diseases and many more.

Adrak ka Raita

(ginger- a virtual medicine chest)

For 4 persons

Ingredients	Quantity
• Adrak (Ginger)	10-15 gms
• Curd	03 cup
• Water	100 ml
• Salt	To taste
• Black Salt	To taste
• Green Chillies	01 no.
• Black Pepper Powder	¼ tea spoon
• Oil	1 tea spoon
• Coriander Leaves	Few sprigs

Method:

➤ Mix curd, well, with water, salt, black salt, half of black pepper.

➤ Wash and finely chop green chillies.

➤ Add half of the chopped green chillies with curd mixture.

➤ Wash and peel ginger.

➤ Finely chop or crush ginger.

➤ Heat oil in a pan and fry ginger till light brown in colour.

➤ Remove from fire and add the curd mixture.

➤ Put lid and leave till cool.

➢ Serve garnished with remaining black Pepper powder and chopped coriander leaves.

Variation: dry powdered ginger may be used instead of fresh ginger.

Note: improves the absorption and assimilation of essential nutrients in the body.

Adrak aur Lahsun ka Raita

(two beneficial herbs coming together)

For 4 persons

Ingredients	Quantity
• Adrak (Ginger)	10 gms
• Lahsun (Garlic)	2-3 flakes
• Curd	03 cup
• Water	100 ml
• Salt	To taste
• Black Salt	To taste
• Green Chillies	01 no.
• Black pepper	¼ tea spoon
• Oil	1 tea spoon
• Coriander Leaves	Few sprigs

Method:

➢ Mix curd, well, with water, salt, black salt, half of black pepper.

➢ Wash and finely chop green chillies.

➢ Add half of the chopped green chillies with curd mixture.

➢ Peel garlic flakes.

➢ Finely chop or crush garlic.

➢ Wash and peel ginger.

➢ Finely chop or crush ginger.

➤ Heat oil in a pan and fry and ginger and garlic till light brown in colour.

➤ Remove from fire and add the curd mixture.

➤ Put lid and leave till cool.

➤ Serve garnished with remaining black Pepper powder and chopped coriander leaves.

Note: effective in fighting infections, preventing cancer and reducing inflammation.

Sweet-Corn Raita

(a healthy addition to the diet)

For 4 persons

Ingredients	Quantity
• Sweet-Corn	50 gm
• Curd	03 cup
• Water	100 ml
• Salt	To taste
• Black Salt	To taste
• Green Chillies	01 no.
• Powdered Red Chillies	¼ tea spoon
• Coriander Leaves	Few sprigs

Method:

➤ Boil sweet corn in prescribed water till tender.

➤ Leave to cool and strain.

➤ Reserve water.

➤ Mix curd, well, with salt, black salt, half of powdered red chillies.

➤ Wash and finely chop green chillies.

➤ Add half of the chopped green chillies with curd mixture.

➤ Add sweet-corn.

➢ Check consistency of raita with reserved water.

➢ Serve garnished with remaining powdered red chillies and chopped coriander leaves.

Note: rich in carbohydrates, protein, fibre and fat

Baby-Corn Raita

(also known as sugar corn)

For 4 persons

Ingredients	Quantity
• Baby-Corn	100 gm
• Curd	03 cup
• Water	100 ml
• Salt	To taste
• Black Salt	To taste
• Green Chillies	01 no.
• Powdered Red Chillies	¼ tea spoon
• Coriander Leaves	Few sprigs

Method:

➢ Drain and wash baby corn.

➢ Cut in small pieces.

➢ Boil in water.

➢ Leave to cool and strain.

➢ Reserve water.

➢ Mix curd, well, with salt, black salt, half of powdered red chillies.

➢ Wash and finely chop green chillies.

➢ Add half of the chopped green chillies with curd mixture.

➢ Mix-in baby corns.

➢ Adjust consistency of raita with reserved water.

➢ Serve garnished with remaining powdered red chillies and chopped coriander leaves.

Note: high in fibre and low in carbohydrates.

Green Chilli Raita

(fiery and healthy raita)

For 4 persons

Ingredients	Quantity
• Green Chillies	03 no.
• Curd	02 cup
• Water	150 ml
• Salt	To taste
• Black Salt	To taste
• Powdered Red Chillies	For garnishing
• Cumin Seeds	½ tea spoon

Method:

➢ Wash and grind green chillies.

➢ Meanwhile, add salt and black salt to the curd and beat curd along with water until smooth.

➢ Roast cumin seeds on hot tawa/pan until nice brown in colour and crush coarsely.

➢ Mix half of the roasted cumin seeds and grinded green chillies in beaten curd.

➢ Serve garnished with remaining roasted cumin seeds.

Variations: A table spoon of sweet imli chutney.

Besan Ka Raita

(true Indian flavour)

For 4 persons

Ingredients	Quantity
• Besan	30 gms.
• Curd	02 cup
• Water	150 ml
• Salt	To taste
• Black Salt	To taste
• Green Chillies	1-2 nos.
• Cumin Seeds	½ tsp
• Powdered Red Chillies	For garnishing
• Cumin Seeds	½ tea spoon

Method:

➢ Roast besan in a dry fry pan till light brown in colour.

➢ Keep aside to cool.

➢ Wash and grind green chillies to make paste.

➢ Make paste of roasted besan with small quantity of water.

➢ Add this paste to remaining water and whisk well to avoid any lump formation.

➢ Mix in salt, black salt, curd and beat until smooth.

➢ Roast cumin seeds on hot tawa/pan until nice brown in colour and crush coarsely.

➤ Mix half of the roasted cumin seeds and grinded green chillies in beaten curd mixture.

➤ Serve chilled garnished with remaining roasted cumin seeds.

Note: rich in proteins and helpful in reducing weight

Sprouted Beans Ka Raita

(benefits are at peak when sprouted)

For 4 persons

Ingredients	Quantity
• Sprouted Beans	50 gms.
• Curd	02 cup
• Water	150 ml
• Salt	To taste
• Black Salt	To taste
• Green Chillies	1-2 nos.
• Powdered Red Chillies	For garnishing
• Cumin Seeds	½ tea spoon

Method:

➢ Wash well the sprouted beans well.

➢ Wash and chop green chillies.

➢ Mix salt, black salt and water with curd and beat until smooth.

➢ Roast cumin seeds on hot tawa/pan until nice brown in colour and crush coarsely.

➤ Mix sprouted beans, half of the roasted cumin seeds and chopped green chillies in beaten curd mixture.

➤ Serve chilled garnished with remaining roasted cumin seeds.

Variations: Sprouted beans may be steamed.

Note: rich sources of proteins, vitamins, moisture, minerals and enzymes

Peanut Raita

(essential for optimum health)

For 4 persons

Ingredients	Quantity
• Peanut (without shell)	30 gms.
• Peanut Butter (Smooth)	50 gms
• Curd	02 cup
• Water	150 ml
• Salt	To taste
• Black Salt	To taste
• Powdered Red Chillies	½ tsp
• Cumin Seeds	½ tsp

Method:

> ➤ Boil peanuts and remove the skin.
> ➤ Coarsely grind boiled peanuts.
> ➤ Mix peanut butter, salt, black salt and half of the powdered red chillies with curd and beat until smooth.
> ➤ Add water and whisk well.
> ➤ Roast cumin seeds on hot tawa/pan until nice brown in colour and crush coarsely.

➢ Grind the cumin seeds, coarsely.

➢ Mix coarsely grounded boiled peanuts and half of the cumin seeds.

➢ Serve chilled garnished with remaining cumin seeds.

Note: rich in energy and good fatty acids

Cornflakes Raita

(a familiar breakfast item)

For 4 persons

Ingredients	Quantity
• Cornflakes	50 gms.
• Curd	02 cup
• Water	150 ml
• Salt	To taste
• Black Salt	To taste
• Powdered Red Chillies	½ tsp
• Cumin Seeds	½ tsp

Method:

➢ Crush Cornflakes.

➢ Mix salt, black salt and half of the powdered red chillies with curd and beat until smooth.

➢ Add water and whisk well.

➢ Roast cumin seeds on hot tawa/pan until nice brown in colour and crush coarsely.

➢ Grind the cumin seeds, coarsely.

➢ Add Cornflakes and half of the cumin seeds. Mix well.

➢ Serve chilled garnished with remaining cumin seeds.

Note: good in reducing fat and enriched in vitamins and minerals.

Muesli Raita

(innovative use of breakfast cereal)

For 4 persons

Ingredients	Quantity
• Muesli	50 gms.
• Curd	02 cup
• Water	150 ml
• Salt	To taste
• Black Salt	To taste
• Powdered Red Chillies	½ tsp
• Cardamom Seeds	¼ tsp

Method:

➢ Coarsely crush muesli.

➢ Mix salt, black salt and half of the powdered red chillies with curd and beat until smooth.

➢ Add water and whisk well.

➢ Coarsely pound cardamom seeds.

➢ Add crushed muesli and half of the pounded cardamom seeds seeds. Mix well.

➢ Serve chilled garnished with remaining cumin seeds.

Note: excessively rich source of insoluble and soluble fiber.

Foot Ka Raita

(an Indian fruit of Melon family)

For 4 persons

Ingredients	Quantity
• Foot	150 gm
• Curd	02 cup
• Water	150 ml
• Salt	To taste
• Black Salt	To taste
• Powdered Red Chillies	½ tsp
• Cumin Seeds	½ tsp

Method:

- ➢ Wash, peel and discard seeds.
- ➢ Chop the flesh.
- ➢ Mix salt, black salt and half of the powdered red chillies with curd and beat until smooth.
- ➢ Add water and whisk well.
- ➢ Roast cumin seeds on hot tawa/pan until nice brown in colour.
- ➢ Grind the cumin seeds, coarsely.
- ➢ Add chopped *foot* and half of the cumin seeds. Mix well.
- ➢ Serve chilled garnished with remaining cumin seeds.

Curry Leaves Raita

(Summers delight)

For 4 persons

Ingredients	Quantity
• Curry Leaves	15-20 grams
• Curd	02 cup
• Water	150 ml
• Salt	To taste
• Black Salt	To taste
• Black Pepper Powder	¼ tea spoon
• Cumin Seeds	½ tea spoon
• Oil	½ tsp

Method:

➢ Wash leaves and drain.

➢ Break or roughly chop leaves.

➢ Add salt, black salt and black pepper powder to the curd and beat curd along with water until smooth.

➢ Roast cumin seeds on hot tawa/pan until nice brown in colour and crush coarsely.

➢ Mix half of the roasted cumin seeds with curd mixture.

➢ Heat oil in a pan and add leaves.

- ➤ Cook for few minutes.
- ➤ Remove form fire and add curd mixture.
- ➤ Serve garnished with remaining roasted cumin seeds.

Note: Very useful for upset stomach.

Whole Spices Raita

(highly appetizing raita)

For 4 persons

Ingredients	Quantity
• Whole Spices Bay Leaf – 1 no., Black pepper -2-3, Cloves -3, cardamom (green and black) -2 each, Cinnamon – 1" stick,	
• Oil	½ tsp
• Curd	02 cup
• Water	150 ml
• Salt	To taste
• Powdered Red chillies	½ tsp
• Black Salt	To taste
• Cumin Seeds	½ tea spoon
• Coriander Leaves	Few sprigs

Method:

➢ Add salt, black salt and half of the powdered red chillies to the curd and beat curd along with water until smooth.

➢ Roast cumin seeds on hot tawa/pan until nice brown in colour.

➢ Mix half of the roasted cumin seeds with curd mixture.

➢ Heat oil in pan.

➢ Add whole spices and cook for 1-2 minutes.

➢ Remove from fire and pour the curd mixture in the pan.

- ➤ Cover and leave to cool.
- ➤ Meanwhile wash green coriander and chop finely.
- ➤ Serve garnished with remaining roasted cumin seeds and chopped coriander leaves.

Note: helpful in digestion.

Cheese Raita

(a delight for vegeterians)

For 4 persons

Ingredients	Quantity
• Cheese	100 gm
• Curd	02 cup
• Water	150 ml
• Salt	To taste
• Powdered Red chillies	½ tsp
• Black Salt	To taste
• Cumin Seeds	½ tea spoon
• Coriander Leaves	Few sprigs

Method:

➢ Roast cumin seeds on hot tawa/pan until nice brown in colour and crush coarsely.

➢ Crush cumin seeds and keep aside.

➢ Wash green coriander and chop finely.

➢ Put the cheese in a blender with 2-3 table spoon of curd and and make a fine paste.

➢ Add remaining curd, water, salt, half of the red chilli powder, black salt and half of the cumin seeds.

➢ Blend well.

> ➤ Serve garnished with remaining red chilli powder, cumin seeds and chopped coriander leaves.

Variations: Cream cheese may be used but adjust the quantity of water and salt.

Note: excellent for gaining weight and rich in calcium content

Pea Raita

(succulent nutritious green seeds)

For 4 persons

Ingredients	Quantity
• Green Peas	100 gm
• Curd	02 cup
• Water	150 ml
• Salt	To taste
• Powdered Red chillies	½ tsp
• Black Salt	To taste
• Cumin Seeds	½ tea spoon
• Coriander Leaves	Few sprigs

Method:

➢ Roast cumin seeds on hot tawa/pan until nice brown in colour and crush coarsely.

➢ Crush cumin seeds and keep aside.

➢ Shell and wash green peas (if using fresh peas).

➢ Wash green coriander and chop finely and keep aside.

➢ Boil peas in water till tender (do not cover).

➢ Drain and reserve water.

➢ Put the peas in a blender with curd and water.

➢ Add water, salt, half of the red chilli powder, black salt and half of the cumin seeds.

➢ Blend well.

➢ Serve garnished with remaining red chilli powder, cumin seeds and chopped coriander leaves.

Note: excellent source of folic, ascorbic acid.

Gulab Ka Raita

(royal raita)

For 4 persons

Ingredients	Quantity
• Rose Petals	15 gm
• Rose water	50 ml
• Curd	02 cup
• Water	70 ml
• Salt	To taste
• Black Salt	To taste
• Green Cardamom Powder	¼ tea spoon

Method:

➢ Mix rose water, curd, water, salt, black salt and green cardamom powder.

➢ Blend well.

➢ Add half of the rose petals and mix.

➢ Serve garnished with remaining rose petals.

Rajmah Raita

(one of the best legumes)

For 4 persons

Ingredients	Quantity
• Rajmah (Kidney Beans)	50 gm
• Curd	02 cup
• Water	150 ml
• Salt	To taste
• Powdered Red chillies	½ tsp
• Black Salt	To taste
• Cumin Seeds	½ tea spoon
• Coriander Leaves	Few sprigs

Method:

➤ Roast cumin seeds on hot tawa/pan until nice brown in colour and crush coarsely.

➤ Crush cumin seeds and keep aside.

➤ Wash red kidney beans.

➤ Wash green coriander and chop finely and keep aside.

➤ Boil beans in water till tender.

➤ Drain and reserve water.

➤ Put beans in a blender with curd and water.

➤ Add water, salt, half of the red chilli powder, black salt and half of the cumin seeds.

➢ Blend well.

➢ Serve garnished with remaining red chilli powder, cumin seeds and chopped coriander leaves.

Note: full of potassium, magnesium, iron and protein

Bamboo Shoots Raita

(a very off beat raita)

For 4 persons

Ingredients	Quantity
• Bamboo Shoots	70 gm
• Curd	02 cup
• Water	150 ml
• Salt	To taste
• Green Chillies	1-2 no
• Black Pepper Powder	¼ tea spoon
• Black Salt	To taste
• Cumin Seeds	½ tea spoon

Method:

➢ Roast cumin seeds on hot tawa/pan until nice brown in colour and crush coarsely.

➢ Crush cumin seeds and keep aside.

➢ Wash and chop green chillies.

➢ Wash bamboo shoots.

➢ Boil these in water till tender.

➢ Drain and discard water.

➢ Chop bamboo shoots.

➢ Put bamboo shoots in a blender with curd and water.

➢ Add water, salt, half of the chopped green chillies, black salt and half of the cumin seeds.

➢ Blend well.

➢ Serve garnished with remaining green chillies, and cumin seeds.

Note: contain vitamins such as vitamin A, B6, E, folate and pantothenic acid. Minerals include calcium, magnesium, phosphorous, potassium, sodium, zinc, copper, manganese, selenium and iron

Mushroom Raita

(Whatever your favourite—crimini, enoki, oyster,
portobello, shiitake or white button)

For 4 persons

Ingredients	Quantity
• Edible Mushrooms	50-70 gm
• Curd	02 cup
• Water	150 ml
• Salt	To taste
• Green Chillies	1-2 no
• Black Pepper Powder	¼ tea spoon
• Black Salt	To taste
• Cumin Seeds	½ tea spoon

Method:

- ➤ Roast cumin seeds on hot tawa/pan until nice brown in colour and crush these coarsely.
- ➤ Crush cumin seeds and keep aside.
- ➤ Wash and chop green chillies.
- ➤ Wash mushrooms.
- ➤ Boil these in water till tender.
- ➤ Drain and discard water.
- ➤ Put mushrooms in a blender with curd and water.

- ➤ Add water, salt, half of the chopped green chillies, black salt and half of the cumin seeds.
- ➤ Blend well.
- ➤ Serve garnished with remaining green chillies, and cumin seeds.

Note: contain selenium and produce vitamin D when exposed to sunlight. Oyster mushrooms are a good source or iron & low in calories

Pakode Ka Raita

(raita of a popular snacks)

For 4 persons

Ingredients	Quantity
• Assorted Pakodas	100 gm
• Curd	02 cup
• Water	150 ml
• Salt	To taste
• Green Chillies	1-2 no
• Red Chilli Powder	¼ tea spoon
• Black Salt	To taste
• Cumin Seeds	½ tea spoon
• Green Coriander	A few sprigs

Method:

➢ Roast cumin seeds on hot tawa/pan until nice brown in colour and crush these coarsely.

➢ Crush cumin seeds and keep aside.

➢ Wash and chop green chillies.

➢ Wash green coriander and chop finely and keep aside.

➢ Blend pakodas in a blender with curd and water.

➤ Add water, salt, half of the chopped green chillies, black salt and half of the cumin seeds.
➤ Blend well.
➤ Serve garnished with remaining green chillies, cumin seeds and chopped coriander raita.

Chips Ka Raita

(Children special)

For 4 persons

Ingredients	Quantity
• Chips	80 gm
• Curd	02 cup
• Water	150 ml
• Salt	To taste
• Green Chillies	1-2 no
• Red Chilli Powder	¼ tea spoon
• Black Salt	To taste
• Cumin Seeds	½ tea spoon

Method:

➢ Roast cumin seeds on hot tawa/pan until nice brown in colour and crush these coarsely.

➢ Crush cumin seeds and keep aside.

➢ Wash and chop green chillies.

➢ Wash green coriander and chop finely and keep aside.

➢ Reserve few chips for garnishing and crush rest coarsely. Keep aside.

➢ Mix curd with water, salt, half of the chopped green chillies, black salt and half of the cumin seeds.

➢ Blend well.

➢ Add crushed chips and mix carefully.

➢ Serve garnished with chips, remaining green chillies, and cumin seeds.

Variations: *Kurkure or corn chips* may also be used.

Chaat Papdi Ka Raita

(again a raita made out of a popular Indian snacks)

For 4 persons

Ingredients	Quantity
• Chaat Papdi	80 gm
• Curd	02 cup
• Water	150 ml
• Salt	To taste
• Green Chillies	1-2 no
• Red Chilli Powder	¼ tea spoon
• Black Salt	To taste
• Cumin Seeds	½ tea spoon

Method:

➢ Roast cumin seeds on hot tawa/pan until nice brown in colour and crush these coarsely.

➢ Crush cumin seeds and keep aside.

➢ Wash and chop green chillies.

➢ Wash green coriander and chop finely and keep aside.

➢ Reserve few chaat papdi for garnishing and crush rest, coarsely. Keep aside.

➢ Mix curd with water, salt, half of the chopped green chillies, black salt and half of the cumin seeds.

➤ Blend well.

➤ Add crushed papdi and mix carefully.

➤ Serve garnished with papdi, remaining green chillies, and cumin seeds.